T0056709

THE STAIRWELL

THE STAIRWELL

MICHAEL LONGLEY

WAKE FOREST UNIVERSITY PRESS

First North American edition

Copyright © Michael Longley, 2014

ISBN 978-1-930630-69-7 (paperback)
Library of Congress Card Number 2014943776

Designed and set in
Lapture and Dante by
Nathan W. Moehlmann,
Goosepen Studio & Press

Printed on acid-free paper
in the United States of America

Wake Forest University Press
Post Office Box 7333
Winston-Salem, NC 27109
WFUPRESS.WFU.EDU

∞∞∞∞∞∞∞∞∞∞∞∞∞∞∞∞∞∞∞∞∞∞

The editors dedicate this
North American edition to
EDWIN G. WILSON,
PROVOST EMERITUS *and*
PROFESSOR OF ENGLISH,
with gratitude and affection.

∞∞∞∞∞∞∞∞∞∞∞∞∞∞∞∞∞∞∞∞∞∞

for

MICHAEL VINEY

Now that the Owennadornaun has disappeared
For you and me where our two townlands meet,
The peaty water takes the long way round
Through Morrison's fields and our imaginations.

CONTENTS

PART TWO

For Peter, My Twin

PART ONE

Hap the blanket round me
And tuck in a flower

W. S. Graham

THE STAIRWELL

for Lucy McDiarmid

I have been thinking about the music for my funeral —
Liszt's transcription of that Schumann song, for instance,
'Dedication' — inwardness meets the poetry of excess —
When you lead me out of your apartment to demonstrate
In the Halloween-decorated lobby the perfect acoustic
Of the stairwell, and stand among pumpkins, cobwebby
Skulls, dancing skeletons, and blow kisses at the ceiling,
Whistling Great War numbers — 'Over There', 'It's a Long,
Long Way', 'Keep the Home Fires Burning' (the refrain) —
As though for my father who could also whistle them,
Trench memories, your eyes closed, your head tilted back,
Your cheeks filling up with air and melody and laughter.
I hold the banister. I touch your arm. Listen, Lucy,
There are songbirds circling high up in the stairwell.

DEATHBED

I imagine my deathbed like my friends' love bed
Whose friends come into the house for breakfast
Every morning, robins, one long-legged, fleet,
The original, another lurking in a corner,
One searching under the bed for spiders,
One swooping from doorway to cheese-dish.

When I die I shall give them all their names.
There will be many robin generations
Coming into the house, and wrens and blackbirds
And long-tailed tits will learn from the robins
About the cheese-dish and saucer of water.
I'll leave the window open for my soul-birds.

ABSENCE

Dear old brother-in-law, I've flown home
Across the Atlantic. I'm far away, but you
Forget. So, yes, I've just gone shopping.
I'll reappear soon at the French window.

NOTEBOOK

I

Why did I never keep a notebook
That filled up with reed buntings
And blackcaps and chiffchaffs, their
Songs a subsong between the lines?

Early April. I am seventeen.
Under an overhanging whin bush
I have spotted linnets building.
A robin has laid her first egg.

II

I find dead on her nest
A lapwing, beneath her
Three perfect eggs, and one
Without shell or colour
That bursts when I touch it.

Her mate sky-suspended
Screaming around my head
Swoops as though to blind me
When I take her in my hands
And look at her torn hole.

III

Who was the professor who took me
Mackerel-fishing off Killard Point?
A marine biologist, he taught me
To brain fish against the gunwales.

On the raised beach I picked out
From pebbles a plover's egg:
It cracked in my trouser pocket
Like a chilly ejaculation.

MALLARD

The mallard, terror-stricken,
Doesn't fly but, slow enough
For her peeping ducklings,
Her body flat to the ground,
Waddles away from me
Where the Owennadornaun
Used to flow, her profile
Imitating Inishturk
Duck-like on the horizon.

STOAT

A wall ripple (drystone
Wall) gable cascade
(Roofless at Dooaghtry)
Machair assassin
Sucking oxygen through
A hole in the throat,
Leaves (near Allaran) a
Rabbit flabbergasted.

ASHES

I

The first creature I meet when I arrive
Is a stoat slipping underneath the gate,
Dominating the garden's quietude,
A part now of my Carrigskeewaun home
From home, standing upright to greet me,
Its white belly a wintry glimpse, ermine.

II

Looking for a second marsh helleborine
Takes me along the perimeter fencing
To where I want my ashes wind-scattered.
Lapwings flap away over Lackakeely.
I'll picture them tonight among yellow flags,
Their heads tucked in, fidgeting as they sleep.

III

Always I think it is the last summer,
My lifetime adrift between the stepping stones
With the badger drowned at spring tide, and past
All that is left of the burial mound.
I am listening with Joe O'Toole's ghost
To the breakers' roar for weather news.

PAINTINGS

I

Gerard Dillon painted the blinds in his two-up,
Two-down house in Clonard Street — Irish saints,
Farm animals, Connemara dreams — so that
At evening when the gas lights were lit and
The blinds drawn, children from the Lower Falls
Would gather to gaze at a magic lantern.

II

Dillon found two wells on Inishlacken,
One cup-sized in a rock, seaweed-thatched,
One at low tide, sandy drinking water.

III

He painted the island like a seabird's nest.

SALAMANDER

Do you remember me turning over a stone
That stayed wet beside the skinny waterfall,
And showing you, when you were a girl,
A sleepy stone-coloured salamander?

Can you startle it, now you are a woman,
And make of it a shipwrecked golden creature,
Its three rubies quenched by sea dark, its empty
Six holes filling up with sand and sea water?

TWO OTTERS

She toddles to the lake without a name,
Your two-year-old, and watches an otter,
Her first otter, half-expected by you
Because, when you were expecting her,
You last watched an otter from this spot,
Your body a holt for otter and child.

ANOTHER WREN

I want to leave to you,
My grandchildren,
This wren from Down,
Its cotton-wool soul,
Wire skeleton, feathers
Apparently alive,
Its tumultuous
Aria in C or
Whatever the key
In which God exists.

MAISIE AT DAWN

Wordless in dawnlight
She talks to herself,
Her speech-melody
A waterlily budding.

AMELIA'S POEM

Amelia, your newborn name
Combines with the midwife's word
And, like smoke from driftwood fires,
Wafts over the lochside road
Past the wattle byre — hay bales
For ponies, Silver and Whisper —
Between drystone walls' river-
Rounded moss-clad ferny stones,
Through the fenceless gate and gorse
To the flat erratic boulder
Where otters and your mother rest,
Spraints black as your *meconium*,
Fish bones, fish scales, shitty sequins
Reflecting what light remains.

FETLOCKS

I had thought of wind-chimes
To accompany your sleep,
But they are too airy, so
I imagine the fetlocks
Of a neighbour's Clydesdale,
Icicles in harsh weather
Tinkling at each earthy stride.

CRY

Your cry translates greylag-geese alarms
And, invisible out there in sea mist,
The prawn-fisherman's puttering outboard.

BIRTH-BED

I waken in the bed where you were born
Weeks ago: the March light from Avernish
Kindles in leafless self-seeded saplings
Water-sparks, and rinses the scallop shells
And white horseshoe that decorate the porch.

This is my unassuming *nunc dimittis*
While I wait like Simeon to cradle you
Swaddled in light and shadow — vernix
And lanugo — even the wattle byre's
Rusty corrugated-iron roof's ablaze.

BLIZZARD

The sheep farmers of Antrim and Down are weeping
For their ewes and spring lambs buried deep in the snow:
The nearest they'll get to a thaw on the cold hills
Are the breath-holes, before these too fill up with snow.

HAIKU

During the power-cut
Maisie wondered: 'Where is me?
I have disappeared.'

SIBELIUS, 1956

An iceberg in the dark
Where we kiss, my bristly
Chin reddening her chin.

She's a rock-'n'-roller.
I want to share with her
Symphonic fragments

Snowdrifting towards their
Theme. She sits on my knee
After a sixth-form hop:

Plastic necklace, bangles
That icicle-tinkle,
Sugar-stiff petticoats'

Rustling aroma. 'Oh,
It's a whole new world
Down there,' a friend says:

Birdcalls in her throat, flute
Notes, our finlandia,
Piccolo passerines.

MICHAELMAS, 1958

I lodged above a poetry library, all
The Irish poets accumulating on Victor
Leeson's shelves in Dublin's Wellington Road,
Reflections in his shiny baby grand.

Bach preludes, Pears toilet soap, bacon smells,
My melancholy first Michaelmas Term,
Cycling to rediscover Nausicaa
In Stanford's class, Odysseus hiding his sex.

Over breakfast Victor said nothing at all
And I had little to say. 'Two eggs please.'
No poetry yet, none of that craziness,
Calypso, Penelope, where were the girls?

Greek Verse Composition and Latin Prose,
Conundrums, three-dimensional crossword
Puzzles, I banged my head. 'The beautiful
Things are difficult,' Stanford quoted.

The Latin love-elegy came true for me
Eventually, when I held her hand
During *Les Enfants du Paradis*
In the Astor cinema along the quays.

Fifty years later, in the catalogue
Of Victor Leeson's poetry books, I find
Like a digamma my name, and we talk
In silence over the breakfast table.

MARIGOLDS, 1960

You are dying. Why do we fight?
You find my first published poem —
'Not worth the paper it's printed on,'
You say. *She gave him marigolds* —

You are dying. 'They've cut out my
Wheesht — I have to sit down
To *wheesht* — like a woman' —
Marigolds *the colour of autumn.*

I need to hitchhike to Dublin
For Trinity Term. 'I'll take you
Part of the way,' you say,
'And we can talk if you like.'

And we talk and talk as though
We know we are just in time.
'A little bit further,' you say
Again and again, and in pain.

A few miles from Drogheda
You turn the car. We say goodbye
And you drive away slowly
Towards Belfast and your death.

To keep in his cold room. Look
At me now on the Newry Road
Standing beside my rucksack. Och,
Daddy, look in your driving mirror.

BOAT

for Seamus

What's the Greek for boat,
You ask, old friend,
Fellow voyager
Approaching Ithaca —
Oh, flatulent sails,
Wave-winnowing oars,
Shingle-scrunching keel —
But, so close to home,
There's a danger always
Of amnesiac storms,
Waterlogged words.

19 July 2011

PSALM

One wreath had blackberry clusters
Intertwined. Was it a blackbird
Or wren that briefly sang a graveside
Aria, godlike in its way, a psalm?
(He will defend you under his wing.
You will be safe under his feathers.)

5 October 2013

THE BROIGHTER BOAT

for Marie

A friend wears as a brooch
Gold boat, golden oars,
Refinement intensified
Below her breastbone,

Mast, oars, tiller
Hammered thin as ash
Keys, sycamore wings,
Rowlocks whispering,

Her journey's replica
With me a stowaway,
A transubstantial
Imaginary oarsman.

25 January 2012

CONSTELLATIONS

poem ending with a line of Dermot Healy

Thistledown and meteors are streaming
Along the lazybeds of the constellations.

FRAGRANT ORCHID

for Catriona & Nic

Your friends lined your daughter's grave with flowers.
May I add belatedly from Carrigskeewaun
Sandwort, just in bloom, and — still in bud —
Grass of parnassus, and lady's bedstraw
That, out of the wind, grows taller, eyebright,
Ragged-robin, saxifrage, bog cotton,
Bog asphodel and speedwell speedwell . . .
At the lake without a name I leave unpicked
One fragrant orchid for her to kneel and sniff.

WATERBIRDS

for Emily

Out of the huge sadness of the *Iliad*
(I was reading Book Fifteen when you died)
Waterbirds are calling — barnacle geese,
Grey herons and long-necked whooper swans —
Waterbirds in flight over a water-meadow,
Honking, settling in front of one another,
Proud of their feather-power — taking me back
To the camogie pitch where your heart failed.
Waterbirds are calling — barnacle geese,
Grey herons and long-necked whooper swans.

WOOD ANEMONES

I

Our beech tree overshadows the hawthorn
And laburnum in Claude Field's back garden,
So he who feeds the fox, and for the badger
Cuts holes in hedges, joins me to witness
The tree surgeon high in the canopy
Deadwooding two (or is it three) hundred years.

II

Claude Field's wood anemones look cheerful
Under the cherry tree: it has taken them
His lifetime to reach across his garden
To our neighbourly hedge: at ninety-three
He shares another year's wood anemones
With me: grandmother's nightcap, windflower.

PADLOCKS

I

Along the iron footbridge to the cathedral
Lovers in their hundreds over the years
Have fastened padlocks — Porky and Pils,
Magda and Jerzy — the names and dates
Scratched with a penknife — the keys tossed
Over their shoulders into the Oder
To twinkle like minnows.
                       We have to stand.
Out of this huge attentive congregation
Some for sure have padlocked their betrothals.
The homily in Polish seems endless.
The one word we understand is 'Eichmann'.
There are shield-bugs mating beyond the bridge.
Does he keep an eye on rusty marriages,
Christ the locksmith in his lofty workshop?

II

After dumplings on cardboard plates
We leave the botanical gardens
For the windy riverside walk
And try to avoid treading on
Amorous shield-bugs — hundreds
Along the pavement — minuscule
Honeymooners — greyish with spots
Valentine red — cherry blossom
Covering motionless passion
With bridal sheets — tipsy gods
We walk hand in hand slowly
To protect from our clumsiness
Love-making on this April day —
Bugs connected bum to bum.

AFTER MIKHAIL LERMONTOV

1. *Night-Walk*

I come out alone onto the boreen,
A flinty path glimmering through mist,
Stilly night, wilderness listening to God,
The constellations in conversation,

Astonishing things up there in the sky,
The earth dozing in pale-blue radiance.
Why, then, am I so downhearted? What
Am I waiting for? What do I regret?

I've stopped expecting anything from life,
I don't feel nostalgic about the past,
I long for freedom and tranquillity,
I long for forgetfulness and sleep,

But not the grave's spine-chilling coma.
I would prefer to fall asleep for ever
With the life force snoozing in my breast
As it rises and falls imperceptibly,

Night and day a kind voice soothing my ears
With affectionate lullabies about love
And over me, green for eternity,
A shadowy oak leaning and rustling.

II. *Homeland*

O my County Mayo home-from-home-land —
What would my neighbours, such understated
Smallholders, make of this grandiloquence?
Paddy Ruane, barbed-wire virtuoso
Who fleeces his ewes with hand-worked shears
(Close to his gateway marsh-cinquefoil hides);
Seamus Henaghan who built his house, box-
Player, lobster-fisherman (will he take me
To bracken-smothered Inishdeigil where,
Before Carrigskeewaun, the O'Tooles lived?)
And Paddy Morrison, his silage boozy
Under black plastic and old tractor tyres,
Stubble yellowing (his most precious crop
Those butterfly orchids on their hummock);
Stonechat fledglings on the telephone wires,
Pebbly voices above the reeds that cover
The 'Liable to Flooding' sign; the ghost
River, my Owennadornaun diverted
Beyond the water-meadow and memory
And the usefulness of the stepping stones
Across the channel; and the sandy slabs
(All that is left of the burial mound);
Horse-mushroom circles and rabbit holes
On the inevitable long-winded trudge
Up the path to my blustery lodging
Between two lakes Mweelrea overshadows,
The ceilidh-house of the thirteen O'Tooles —
O my County Mayo home-from-home-land!

INSOMNIA

Accompany me on insomnia's walk
Around Carrigskeewaun — my synapses
Are sheeptracks — to where the footling waterfall
Takes two steps down to the saltmarsh
Beside our boulder-seat.
                              In the asylum
Helen Thomas took Ivor Gurney's hand
When he was miles away from Gloucestershire
And sanity, and on Edward's county map
Guided his lonely finger down the lanes.
You are like Helen Thomas. Take my hand.

WILD RASPBERRIES

Following the ponies' hoof-prints
And your own muddy track, I find
Sweet pink nipples, wild raspberries,
A surprise among the brambles.

LIZARD ORCHID

I

All ears in the Mugello
What with the far cuckoo,
The harmonising frog
And crickets everywhere,
Domestic sounds as well —
Heidi baking a chestnut
Cake, Lorenzo's ladder
Scraping the cherry tree —
We find in Silvano's
Sloping upper meadow
Close to the wood, regal
Among seeding grasses,
An orchid, each lower lip
A streamer, extroversion
Requiring subtle breezes,
A name to silence cuckoo
And frog, lizard orchid.

II

Did the muddy boots of Tommies
Really bring back to England
From the Great War lizard-orchid
Seeds — stalks taller than you'd think,
Tongues little-finger-long, ribbons
For widow hats — dead soldiers
Returning, adhesive souls?

MUD TURF

He remembered at Passchendaele
Where men and horses drowned in mud,
His bog apprenticeship, mud turf,
Shovelling mud up out of the drain
Onto the bank where it was dried:
Mud turf kept the home fires burning.

BOY-SOLDIER

The spear-point pierces his tender neck.
His armour clatters as he hits the ground.
Blood soaks his hair, bonny as the Graces',
Braids held in place by gold and silver bands.
Think of a smallholder who rears a sapling
In a beauty spot a burn burbles through
(You can hear its music close to your home)
Milky blossoms quivering in the breeze.
A spring blizzard blows in from nowhere
And uproots it, laying its branches out.
Thus Euphorbus, the son of Pantheus,
A boy-soldier — the London Scottish, say,
The Inniskillings, the Duke of Wellington's —
Was killed and despoiled by Menelaus.

SECOND LIEUTENANT TOOKE

I should have commemorated before now
Second Lieutenant Tooke who helped my dad
Rescue Nurse Moussett of the French Red Cross
At Paris Plage in June nineteen-seventeen.

He was swept away by currents and drowned.
My life-saving dad just made it to the shore.
Not once did he mention the unlucky Tooke.
This was a breather before Passchendaele.

RONALD COLMAN

My dad served with Ronald Colman in the Great War
And laughed at his daydream of Hollywood stardom.
London-Scottish kilts looked frumpish after battle,
Blood, mud and shit bespattering handsome knees.
My dad lost all his teeth before he was twenty
And envied Ronald Colman's spectacular smile.
He watched him trimming his moustache in cold tea
At a cracked mirror, a thin black line his trademark.
Wounded at Messines — shrapnel in his ankle —
He tried in his films to cover up his limp — *Beau
Geste, Lost Horizon* — my dad would go to see them all.
Did he share a last Woodbine with Ronald Colman
Standing on the firestep, about to go their separate
Ways, over the top, into No Man's Land, and fame?

AT HIGH WOOD

I picture my gentle dad at High Wood
Lying wounded among the splintered trees
And unburied dead, some of them his mates,
Some his victims, shot and bayoneted:
Many Trojans and Achaeans fell that day
And lay side by side, faces in the mud.

THE HORSES OF RHESUS

Odysseus yanked corpses by the ankle
And cleared a path for the horses of Rhesus:
They were whiter than snow and wind-speedy
And wavy-maned and very beautiful
And unused to treading on dead soldiers.

LUNCH

I

Missiles find their mark,
On both sides soldiers fall
(Mutual wounds) but
The Greeks break through
At that time of day
When the woodcutter,
His arms exhausted
From chopping trees,
His stomach rumbling,
Prepares his lunch.

II

Field-kitchen smells,
Memories of home
Between explosions —
Dad, can that be you
Rattling your mess-tin
And bellyaching
About the bully beef
As the Germans advance?
Here is an apple
Wrapped in tranquillity.

FACE

Idomeneus takes perfect aim
And hits Erymas in the mouth
And the spear penetrates the brain
And splits the white bones, and the teeth
Blow out and from the eye-sockets
Blood squirts and open-mouthed he
Vomits blood from lips and nostrils
And death's black cloud encloses him.

Homer gets no nearer than this
To the anonymous Tommy,
His human face blasted away.
What can surviving hands reach up
To touch? Tongue-stump? Soul-meat?
Homer's ghost has nothing to say.

THE TIN NOSES SHOP

Give us golden masks, eyebrows and eyelids
Hammered out of gold, and Schliemann claiming
'I have gazed on the face of Agamemnon.'

GLASS BOX

for Bel Mooney

Imagine a shallow glass box
About nine inches by seven,
She writes, a bundle of papers
Inside, tied with brown ribbon,
Photos of our battlefield trip
Interleaved with war poems
She has copied out in longhand.
A shrapnel ball (in cellophane
For protection) nestles there
And rusty shrapnel casing
And the chestnuts and acorns
We examine in one photo.
In another, under a cross,
What can we be looking at?
Embroidered postcards evoke
Men who fought and loved and died,
She says. I who wrote the poems
Imagine a shallow glass box.

GRASSHOPPERS

Should I join them
The old fellas
Above Troy's gate
Demobbed by age
Their fighting days
Long behind them
Good talkers still
Conversation
Like tree-crickets
Or grasshoppers
Settled on branches
Deep in a wood
Voices gently
Lilting lily-like?

PRIVATE UNGARETTI

after Mark Thompson: a found poem

The reprieve from danger
Cast a halo around
Sunlight on dewy grass,
Purple shadow thrown
By mountains, the carnal
Pink of sunset, a green
Glade amid blitzed woodlands
Above the Isonzo.
                 We
Hear the din of battle
In the white silence
Around his words.

A PEBBLE

Kneeling he lays on Isaac
Rosenberg (his uncle)'s headstone
A pebble, a paperweight
Holding down the poems.

For him and the other pilgrims
I read aloud 'Dead Man's
Dump', one of the greatest
Poems in the world, I say.

Is he really buried here?
His face keeps reappearing
(His nephew with a pebble)
His long sad Treblinka face.

HAILSTONES

at the Memorial to the Murdered Jews of Europe, Berlin

It must have been God or, rather, Yahweh
Who scattered the granite slabs with hailstones
And threw them from His hand so accurately
Not one Jew was uncommemorated.

OGHAM

a keyboard upended
in the grazing
now that the repertoire
goes underground

PART TWO

For Peter, My Twin

∞∞∞∞∞∞∞∞∞∞∞∞∞∞∞∞∞∞∞∞∞∞∞∞∞∞

Snow is truly a sign of mourning

Giuseppe Ungaretti

THE WHEELCHAIR

Pushing you in your wheelchair to the sea
I look down at your yellowy bald patch
And recall your double-crown's tufty hair.

You were the naughtier twin, were you not?
It was I who wept when you were chastised.
Where am I pushing you, dear brother, where?

THE TREES

I dreamed we were cutting down the trees
Of childhood: at the back of our garden
The grey ash from which we dropped into
The playing fields, two flowering currants'
Summer hum, the cherry tree that after
Many barren years produced five pears,
The sickly apple tree, the beautiful
Poisonous laburnum, and the cypress
That was impossible to climb. Peter,
If you hide in there, I'll never find you.

THE ARROW

You were sunbathing beyond the laburnum's
Shadow when I shot an arrow, steel-
Tipped, feathery, lethal at the zenith.

I shouted and you rolled away from spinal
Paralysis, my brotherly arrow piercing
The groundsheet where your navel had been.

THE STRAY

Three days before you died
One of your cats, Milly,
Disappeared, so I said
Into myself this poem,

My translation from Gwen John's
French, a prayer for Milly
To materialise
And lick your cold fingers:

My little cat
Living wild in the wood
Have you forgotten then
Your previous existence

Perhaps you are
Upset with me
But I've tried to understand
All of your little heart

I never felt myself
To be your superior
Small mysterious soul
In the body of a cat

I am so heartbroken
At not seeing you
I've thought of leaving
For the Land of the Dead

But I shall be here
If you come back one day
For I have been comforted
By the God of Love

The day of your funeral
In October sunshine
Milly, not the friendliest
Tabby, came back home.

THE EYE-PATCH

You lifted the corner of your eye-patch
To peep at your twin brother and the world.

You wore it to strengthen your lazy eye.
All your life you worried about your good eye.

Which of your eyes am I trying to close,
Wary of its reptilian expressionlessness?

THE ALPHABET

I taught you the Greek alphabet, Peter:
Xi (ξ) was Zeta (ζ) with its arms folded.
But, too late for imaginary voyages
In wooden boats, you studied metalwork.

A marine engineer on oil tankers, you
Journeyed around the globe, how many times?
I dallied with Nausicaa and Calypso
And set sail without you for Ithaca.

THE FEET

for Catherine

You showed me my twin's feet when he was dead,
Your sailor-husband's feet, your engineer's — how
Cold they felt, how handsome ankle and toe,
Bone-shapes out of our gloomy womb-tangle —
A god's immortal feet, I'll dare to think,
When we scatter his ashes in the North Sea
Off the windy pier at Whitburn Village —
Poseidon, say, who drives his chariot's bronze-
Hoofed horses so headlong over the waves
All the sea-creatures know who it must be
And the sea parts with a kind of happiness
And the axle doesn't even get wet.

THE APPARITION

'Are you asleep, Achilles? Have you forgotten me?
Bury me quickly, please, and let me through Death's
Gates: exhausted ghosts get in the way and keep me
From crossing the River to join them: a lost soul
I sleepwalk on the wrong side of the gateway.
Let me hold your hand: once you've cremated me
I'll never come back again out of the darkness.
Never again will you and I sit down together
To make plans, a discreet distance from our friends.
My birthright, Death's abominable night-terror,
Overwhelms me now: your destiny too is fixed,
God-like Achilles: death below the Trojan walls.
One more request: bury our bones together
In the gold two-handled jar your mother gave you.'

'Patroclus, dear brother, I shall do as you ask:
I'll see to the arrangements for your funeral. But
Come closer now, for a moment let us embrace
And wail in excruciating lamentation.'
He reached out but he couldn't get hold of him:
Like smoke the hallucination slipped away
Bat-squeaking underground. Achilles, thunderstruck,
Threw up his hands and blurted out heartbroken words:
'Even in the House of Death something remains,
A ghost or image, but there's no real life in it.
All night the apparition of sad Patroclus
Has hovered over me, weeping and keening
And giving instructions. Did I imagine him?
He looked so like himself, a double, a twin.'

THE LION

Having left him to fight and die on his own
Achilles laid his hands on Patroclus's chest,
Blood-thirsty hands, guilty lamentation —
Like a lion, heartbroken when he finds
His neglected cubs snatched from their thicket
By deer-hunters, and goes on a shaggy
Rampage through glen after glen to track them down.
(Remember the lion at Bellevue Zoo, Peter,
Paws crossed, gazing out over Belfast Lough?)

THE BAY

You'd have loved the funeral games, Peter
— Sports-crazy, our Patroclus, a true Greek —
The chariot race, squabbles about the spoils,
One horse in particular, out in front,
A bay, reddish brown all over except for
The blaze on his forehead, round as the moon.

THE STALLION

Let's go back to the riding field
In Bristow Park when we were boys
And GIs trotted, after the War,
In a muddy figure of eight,
And watch from behind a hawthorn
Patroclus harnessing Xanthus
And Balius, Achilles' wind-swift
Horses (out of Storm-Filly by
Western Gale when she was grazing
In Lagan Meadows, near Ocean
Stream) alongside Pedasus,
A perfectly ordinary stallion
But fast as that immortal pair,
A suitable mount for you or me.

THE FOALS

Wherever you are, you can find the space
For thousands of mares and their glossy foals
Grazing the water-meadow in family groups.
The North Wind falls in love with two or three
And, disguised as a black-maned stallion,
Blows in off the North Sea and impregnates
— How many mares would you say? — the result
In any case, my dear twin, is twelve foals
(And it's these I want to tell you about —
Isn't there a cornfield close to your house
On the by-road into Whitburn Village?) —
Twelve race-horses in the making, so fast
They will zoom over the top of the harvest
Without breaking a single ear of corn.

THE MULE-CART

An engineer, you would appreciate
The technique for yoking the mule-cart —
When they fasten a wicker basket on top
And take down from its peg a boxwood yoke
With knob and guide-hooks for holding the reins
And bring out the lashing-rope — fourteen feet long —
And settle the yoke on the well-polished pole
And slip the eye of the rope over a peg
And tie the rope three times around the knob
And secure it all the way down the pole
And twist it under a hook and thus yoke
Strong-footed draught-mules to the mule-cart.
(What's the function of the peg exactly?)

THE BASKET

The mule-cart would be ransom-laden
With expensive vessels made of gold
And with skillets, kettles, pots as well,
Cooking utensils the weight of home.

They would trundle to the battlefield
And carry back a fallen soldier,
The mule-cart creaking with its burden,
Bone-basket, corpse-cradle, wicker-work.

THE BOXERS

We were combatants from the start. Our dad
Bought us boxing gloves when we were ten —
Champions like Euryalus, say, or Epeius
Of wooden-horse fame: 'I am the greatest!'
'Nobody's going to knock me down!' Listen,
Peter, to the commentary — gruesome teeth-
Grinding, sweat splattering their arms and legs,
Huge fists in ox-hide thongs slugging it out,
Then the knock-out blow to Euryalus's chin —
Hoisting him with an uppercut — like a fish
That arches out of weed-tangled shallows
And collapses back into hazy water,
Sea wind sending shock-waves up the beach —
The winner gives the loser a helping hand
And his seconds support him across the ring
On dragging feet, head lolling to one side,
Blood clots et cetera et cetera . . .
I'll tie your gloves. Shall we fight again?

THE WRESTLERS

Ajax the super-heavyweight takes on
Tricky Odysseus — strong-arm arm-locks —
Like the gable rafters a good carpenter
Bolts together to wind-proof a high house —
Sweaty vertebrae-cracking backbreakers,
Red weals along shoulders and ribs — scuffles —
Deadlock — the crowd getting bored — until
Ajax lifts Odysseus — who outsmarts him
With a behind-the-knee kick and topples
Over on top of him, and they start again —
But the referee (Achilles) stops the fight,
Declares a draw, and leaves them scrapping there —
Not much better than you and me, brother.
Like boys really. Prizes for everyone.

THE EAGLE

In the wind and rain at September-end
When the roads to where you lay were flooded,
I might have welcomed the ominous bird
We find in Homer, best of the prophetic
Birds, the black eagle, shadowy hunter
Whose wingspan covers the double-doors
Of the high-roofed bedroom where you die.

THE DOVE

In the improbable archery contest
Does it matter who shoots the first arrow
That snips the dove's tether and sets her free,
The second arrow already on its way
That pierces her — right through — under the wing
As she rises into the overcast sky,
And, fluttering down, she balances — just —
On the mast of one of the dark-prowed ships,
Her feathers droopy, her head hanging low?

THE TWINS

Our representatives in the chariot race
Would have to be the twin Moliones,
Kteatos and Eurytos, Aktor's sons
(Though their real father was Poseidon) —
Siamese twins, joined below the waist,
One grasping the reins for dear life,
The other whipping the horses to win,
Two souls, one well-balanced charioteer
Taking the trophy and this epitaph.

THE BIRTHDAY

This is our first birthday without you,
My twin, July the twenty-seventh.
Where are you now? I'm looking out for you.
Have you been skinny-dipping at Allaran
Where the jellies won't sting, or in the lake
Among the reeds and damsel flies, sandwort
Stars at your feet, grass of parnassus in bud?
This year the residential swans have cygnets,
Four of them. They won't mind you splashing,
Nor will the sandpipers eyeing Dooaghtry
For a nesting place among the pebbles
At the samphire line. Now you know the spot.
Choughs flock high above their acrobatic
Cliff face and call to you antiquated
Expletives *pshaw pshaw pshaw*. Again and
Again I mention the erratic boulder
Because so much happens there, five hares
In the morning, then a squiggle of stoats.
I've boiled organic beetroots for supper.
Will your pee be pink in heaven? Oh,
The infinite gradations of sunset here.
Thank you for visiting Carrigskeewaun.
Don't twist your ankle in a rabbit hole.
I'll carry the torch across the duach.

THE DUCKBOARDS

The longer way round from Carrigskeewaun
Goes past the bottom of the second lake,
Through salt marsh and yellow flags, and over
Rotten duckboards I wouldn't venture on
Except to look for rare helleborines,
The mallard's nest in its grassy well, or
Our father's ghost, as though at Passchendaele,
Teetering on walkways that disappear
As we follow behind him in the rain.

THE FROST

They kept you refrigerated for days, my twin.
I kissed your forehead where the frost was fading.

THE FIRE

I press the button at your funeral.
The curtains close behind your coffin.
Can you hear the wind in high branches
Howling at its angriest, a bellows
That kindles sparks in hillside clearings
And incinerates the whole woodland?

NOTES & ACKNOWLEDGEMENTS

I am deeply indebted to the distinguished Greek scholar Maureen
Alden. It has been a privilege to explore Homer's world in her
company. 'Deathbed' was inspired by the family of robins in Tim
and Mairead Robinson's home in Roundstone, County Galway.

'Paintings' was written to accompany Gerard Dillon's picture
'The Little Green Fields' in an exhibition in the National
Gallery of Ireland and in the accompanying publication
Lines of Vision: Irish Writers on Art (Thames and Hudson).

'Salamander' refers to the gold brooch found with other valuables
in the shipwrecked Spanish galleon Girona (the collection is
housed in the Ulster Museum). A drawing by Sarah Longley,
based on the brooch, accompanied the poem in the exhibition and
subsequent publication, *26 Objects: 4 National Museums* (Unbound).

'Michaelmas, 1958' was written for *Jubilee Lines* (Faber), edited
by Carol Ann Duffy. 'The Broighter Boat' was written for the
anthology *What We Found There: Poets Respond to the Treasures of the
National Museum of Ireland*, edited by Theo Dorgan (Dedalus Press).

'Night-Walk' was written for *After Lermontov: Translations for the
Bicentenary*, edited by Peter France and Robyn Marsack (Carcanet).
Lermontov is the only begetter of 'Homeland', but this poem is
not a translation. 'Lizard Orchid' owes its closing image to Sarah
Raven's remarkable florilegium, *Wild Flowers* (Bloomsbury).

'Mud Turf' and 'Boy-Soldier' were inspired by Thomas
McAlindon's superb family memoir *Two Brothers Two Wars*
(Lilliput). 'Boy-Soldier' was included in *1914: Poetry Remembers*,
edited by Carol Ann Duffy (Faber). 'Second Lieutenant Tooke':
my father's bravery is recorded in the Royal Humane

Society's relevant Case Book (Case no. 43,442). He was awarded the Society's bronze medal. An In Memoriam certificate was sent to Tooke's relations.

'Private Ungaretti' versifies a passage from Mark Thompson's masterly history *The White War: Life and Death on the Italian Front, 1915–1919* (Faber). 'The Stray': I discovered this poem in Sue Roe's fine biography, *Gwen John: A Life* (Viking).

Some words may require a gloss: *townland* is a rural term for an area of land that varies from a few acres to thousands; *machair* is Irish and Scots Gaelic for a sandy plain behind dunes and affording some pasturage; *duach*, the Irish for sandbanks or dunes, means in Mayo the same as *machair*; *yellow flags* are wild irises; *digamma* is a letter from the early Greek alphabet that fell into disuse.

Acknowledgements are due to the following publications in which some of these poems first appeared: *Agenda, Archipelago, Daedalus, Edinburgh Review, Icarus, Irish Times, London Review of Books, The New Yorker, Poetry Ireland Review, Poetry London, Poetry Review, Prairie Schooner, The Shop, The Times Literary Supplement, Yellow Nib*; and also to the BBC and RTE.

I am very grateful to Alexander McCall Smith, thanks to whose generosity and vision my wife and I spent a fulfilling month in Spring 2013 as Joint 'Isabel Dalhousie' Fellows at the Institute for Advanced Studies in the Humanities, University of Edinburgh.

The cover drawing by Sarah Longley depicts the Moliones (Siamese twins) escaping from Nestor. It is based on a Greek vase painting from the Geometric Period: see *Geometric Greece* by J. N. Coldstream (Ernest Benn).

forty-two whoopers call
then the echoes
as though there are more swans
over the ridge